MW00352275

OBEDIENCE TRAINING

HEEL **DOWN**

DOGS QUARTERLY

by Dennis Kelsey-Wood

Obedience training isn't simply about getting your dog to do something when you ask him to, it's about learning to communicate with your dog. By training your dog in short, easy lessons, you'll develop a shared vocabulary. When you say "Sit," "Down," "Stay"—even "Roll Over"—he'll know what you mean because you've taken the time to teach him. He'll also learn to listen to you and to look to you for instruction and leadership. When this happens, not only will you enjoy your dog more, but he'll be happier, too, because dogs need a pack leader. So read this book and start "schooling" your dog, strengthening your position as pack leader, and working as a team, and soon you and your dog will be communicating better than ever.

© by T.F.H. Publications, Inc.

Distributed in the UNITED STATES to the Pet Trade by T.F.H. Publications, Inc., One T.F.H. Plaza, Neptune City, NJ 07753; on the Internet at www.tfh.com; in CANADA Rolf C. Hagen Inc., 3225 Sartelon St. Laurent-Montreal Quebec H4R 1E8; Pet Trade by H & L Pet Supplies Inc., 27 Kingston Crescent, Kitchener, Ontario N2B 2T6; in ENGLAND by T.F.H. Publications, PO Box 15, Waterlooville PO7 6BQ; in AUSTRALIA AND THE SOUTH PACIFIC by T.F.H. (Australia), Pty. Ltd., Box 149, Brookvale 2100 N.S.W., Australia; in NEW ZEALAND by Brooklands Aquarium Ltd. 5 McGiven Drive, New Plymouth, RD1 New Zealand; in SOUTH AFRICA, Rolf C. Hagen S.A. (PTY.) LTD. P.O. Box 201199, Durban North 4016, South Africa; in Japan by T.F.H. Publications, Japan—Jiro Tsuda, 10-12-3 Ohjidai, Sakura, Chiba 285, Japan. Published by T.F.H. Publications, Inc.

MANUFACTURED IN THE
UNITED STATES OF AMERICA
BY T.F.H. PUBLICATIONS, INC.

Your puppy looks to you for fair leadership and affection so she can grow up to be a well-mannered family member.

CONTENTS

Eileen Robinson works with her Golden Retriever, Thornfield's Mister Mario, CD, on the sit and stay commands.

Photography: Isabelle Francais, Tara Darling, W. De Veer, Alice Pantfoeder, Judith Strom, Karen Taylor.

Once upon a time dogs were bred to perform definite functions, but today they're bred primarily as companions. That means it's up to their owners to give them a "job" by training them.

INTRODUCTION

Over the years, dogs have been trained to fulfill a number of functions and have been selectively bred with those functions in mind. In the past, there were practical reasons for keeping dogs, and the dogs' minds were fully occupied with carrying out their duties. As more people began to keep dogs simply for the pleasure of having them around, the dog started to become a problem in human society. Without having a need to use his brain for functional purposes, and being owned by someone who had no idea how to control an animal, the problem dog resulted. One of the fundamental mistakes made by many dog owners, and even quite a few trainers, is that they forget that the dog is a wild animal living in a human society.

Although basic dog training is a very straightforward process, the number of poorly trained dogs clearly underlines the fact that many people experience difficulties. For most dog trainers, the problem is not training the dog, but teaching the owner to understand that there is a dog on the other end of the lead, not a human.

Methods of teaching dogs differ depending on the instructor. You must keep an open mind at all times so you can continually add to your knowledge. The best teacher you have is your dog. Study him, watch how he reacts to situations, and especially watch how he reacts to you. If he comes to you at all times with a wagging tail and an obvious desire to reach you quickly, then you are doing just fine.

If he ever starts to be apprehensive about approaching you or he cowers with his tail lowered or between his legs, then you have problems with your approach to training. Never forget that training your dog is a two-way street. You and your dog are a team, and both of you should be happy with the results.

This Border Collie works a flock of sheep as many of his ancestors have done. Herding instinct and ability are inherent in this breed.

Dogs, like this Australian Shepherd, do not lack intelligence, but they do not rationalize the way humans do. Instead, they function on instinct and memory.

THE MIND OF A DOG

A dog's mind is a relatively simple thing. I do not mean that the dog lacks intelligence, but he does not go through life rationalizing his decisions or weighing the moral implications of what he is doing. He is purely concerned about his own welfare. When he has a leader, he will display loyalty.

Training is all about channeling your dog's instincts. This is a Border Terrier retrieving over a high jump.

The dog accepts his leader and does not evaluate the leader's quality. While a good leader will get the very best out of the dog and a bad one will not, both leaders will still get a high degree of loyalty.

INSTINCT AND MEMORY

Apart from his genetic make-up, the two things that shape the dog's mind are his instincts and his memory. These are the two factors you must understand to train your dog.

The first factor, instinct, is a natural urge to take a given course of action without having to think about it. It is an involuntary impulse. It is also any natural skill that an individual is born with. All animals react instinctively to given situations. For example, a strong instinct in dogs is to protect what is important to his survival, including his owner and his owner's property.

Training is all about channeling the dog's instincts into a useful purpose or controlling them so they do not become a danger or a nuisance. You must educate your dog to the order of the pack, which is you and your family. Without proper training, your dog has no option but to "follow his instincts."

The second factor is memory. A dog's memory differs in quality from breed to breed and from dog to dog, just as it differs with human individuals. Generally, a dog's powers of recall are extremely good. A dog may retain a memory, without recall of it, for most of his life and still be able to recall it. An example would be if the dog was separated from a loving owner for a number of years and then met the owner again. The dog will remember because the original impulse put into his memory was very strong.

HOW A DOG LEARNS

A dog learns by using his instincts and memory in conjunction with each other. There are basically three types of memories that a dog will have: passive (neutral), positive (pleasurable), or negative (non-pleasurable). The memory acts as a sort of override mechanism to the instinct. An example is that if a dog sees a cat nearby, his instinct tells him to chase the cat. However, if he meets with a negative consequence every time he chases a cat, his brain will record this. In time, the

The Roar-Hide™ from Nylabone® is an excellent training aid because it's a safe and pleasurable reward. Offer your dog a Roar-Hide™ when you want to praise him for a job well done.

dog's brain will tell the dog that it is not in his best interest to chase the cat, thus the brain overrides the instinct. Obviously, the greater the number of memories, the less chance there is that the dog will need to rely solely on his instincts to guide him in his actions.

A human's brain works in the same way, except that humans can apply logic where dogs cannot. It may appear at times as if the dog is using logic, but as far as we know this is not the case. For example, imagine a long, high wall with a door in it that the dog cannot enter. Initially, the dog will pace back and forth, perhaps whimper, and perhaps attempt to jump over the wall. He may, by trial and error, find that there is an open door around the corner. Upon meeting a similar structure, such as a house, the dog finds that he cannot get in the door. His memory reminds him of the wall, so he quickly begins to look for another door. It may look like logic, but he actually just searched his memory for information.

There is another factor that affects the combination of memory and instinct as it relates to training: a threshold. This is the level of intensity needed to stimulate an action. For example, a Pit Bull Terrier has a high threshold of pain, meaning that he will tolerate a high degree of pain before visibly showing it. A low threshold is the opposite, meaning that it takes little stimulus to prompt an action. This is crucial in the training process, and you must understand it in relation to your dog. The instincts to hunt and chase are examples of very low thresholds in all carnivorous animals—this is why a dog will chase at the drop of a hat.

When training a dog, the memory must be capable of overcoming an instinct or else the instinct will be followed, it really is that simple. The complication is that you cannot know just how powerful an instinct is in a given dog, and thus what level of negative impulse is needed to override the instinct. This is a most important aspect of training.

The best way you can train your dog to cope with many situations is to put him in different situations on a regular basis so that he can become familiar with them. You will then only have to use minimal correctional methods, which will ultimately result in a very steadfast dog. This is where repetition of the earlier learned commands will become effective. Thus, repetition is only of value when it will serve a useful purpose, not when it is used to try and

Because Beagles and other scent hounds have a very low threshold for using their noses, trainers of these breeds will need to be extra creative to get them to heel, for example, without sniffing the ground.

To maximize the effects of training, your dog needs to be healthy and alert—the products of a good diet. A combination of premium vegetables and meat will provide maximum nutrition and palatability insuring healthy eating. Photo courtesy of Nature's Recipe Pet Foods.

There is actually a negative to talking too much to your dog at certain times. The dog listens for your commands and does not need to hear you rambling on incessantly. There is also no need to shout at your dog—he has much better hearing than you do. You should talk quietly, but clearly and soothingly. This has the obvious benefit that when you raise your voice slightly, it carries more conviction if the dog is not paying attention. It is also beneficial

correct a situation that the original training was not intended to cover.

LANGUAGE

Your dog does not understand English, French, Italian, or any other language and he never will. What your dog does understand is tone of voice and length of words. When you say a word, it has its own distinctive tone and length, just as a growl does in the wolf pack. It conveys a meaning in association with facial expressions, body language, and the situation you are in. The dog is intelligent enough to link all of these together and use them to determine your mood and what you expect it to do or not do.

Given this fact, it is obvious that using excessive voice communication has little merit. It doesn't matter what words you use in communicating with your dog, as long as they are consistent and spoken in a tone that is related to a given requirement. You could use the same word for every single command and, as long as you varied your tone and length, the dog would understand every one perfectly.

What your dog hears when you talk to him is only your tone of voice and the length of the words you use. Is this Bull Terrier puppy understanding what his owner is saying?

to train your dog to a whistle. This gives you far greater long-range control, including when you are out of sight.

AFFECTION

Affection is the most important instinct a dog has as far as humans are concerned. Because he is a pack animal, he has a strong desire to want to be in a family unit, whether it is of his own species or a substitute human pack. The stronger the bond he shares with his fellow pack members, the more secure he feels. He wants to please because this means that he will lead a happier life within the pack.

If your dog is given lots of affection and praise, he will naturally feel important. Since he wants that feeling to continue, he will do his best to please you. The danger lies in the fact that as the dog gains confidence, and in the ab-

Dogs love to please their owners, and particularly enjoy playing games with them. This Pekingese puppy plays tug-of-war with his young friend.

Your dog will feel important and will want to work for you if you lavish praise or a favorite toy on him for doing something correctly. This Border Collie gets his Gumabone® Frisbee® for responding to "sit."

sence of a definite code of conduct, he will call on his wild instincts to tell him what to do in given situations. If he knows no difference, he will snap at strangers because he thinks he is doing the right thing for his pack. He may chase cats and cars because chasing is a natural thing to do. If you do not take any negative steps in response to these behaviors, he interprets them as part of his role within your pack.

By correcting the dog when he does wrong by your standards, and lavishing praise on him when he does right, he will obviously want to do right and be praised. He does not stop to analyze why he cannot do this or that, he only focuses on what happens when he does. If he receives much praise, it will create a strong positive impulse. If praise is balanced with fair discipline,

the social order of things will be complete and the dog will be content.

Remember that the key to all dog training is looking at situations through the mind of the dog. You may still not get it all correct when training your dog, but you will start out with an advantage. No trainer is perfect. We all make errors in judgment and so might your dog, but most errors will be on your behalf in not being able to communicate properly. However, as you achieve each new objective, you will become more at one with your dog and will come to understand him a little bit better. Your relationship will grow stronger because your dog will be real part of your life that you have taken time to develop. You will teach but you will also learn, so it will be a true partnership of teamwork built on the hard work and efforts of both of you.

You *and* your dog will be contributing to the training program, so both of you should be eating right. For dogs with dietary sensitivities to other meats, venison is an excellent alternative. Discuss this and other dietary options with your veterinarian. Photo courtesy of Nature's Recipe Pet Foods.

SOCIAL ORGANIZATION IN WILD DOGS

Unless you have some appreciation of how your dog would live in his wild state, it becomes difficult to understand what motivates him or why he reacts the way he does to those around him—you and your family. While it is obvi-

basis of who is the strongest. The minute that the leader is unable to defeat any challenger in the pack, his reign is over.

Beneath the leader there is a hierarchical system, meaning that all of the other pack members have a position in

least as many offspring as are lost. Cubs are thus very important to the wolf pack. As a cub grows, he is educated in the pack order of things. If he takes liberties with adults, he is very promptly put in his place. As he plays with other

Our domesticated canine companions are descended from wolves, which are pack animals.

ously impossible to know exactly how a dog thinks, certain conclusions can be drawn from observations of wild dogs, both as single animals and as members of a pack.

The wolf pack is a highly organized unit that may consist of just three or four individuals, or it may contain thirty or more wolves. The pack is led by what is termed an alpha individual, which may be a male or a female. Leadership is determined on the age-old

descending order of importance. This order is based again on physical strength, as the pack structure is based on survival of the fittest. However, if the leader favors certain individuals, then they may attain a higher status than their own power would otherwise give them—you can see the comparison with human society.

When a she-wolf has cubs, her status may rise because the species is very dependent on the ability to reproduce at

cubs, he will come to appreciate which are his betters. He will see the fights and quarrels that take place between the adults. He copies the adults in what they do, and in this way slowly learns from them.

All members will periodically approach the pack leader to exchange information and generally show their submission to his or her status. The submissive posture for all canids is with their tails between their legs and as low to the ground as possible. In the full submissive posture, the animal rolls onto his back, thus exposing his most vulnerable parts. He may also urinate while in this position.

Although there is quite a lot of fighting within a pack, there is also much tenderness and affection. There is also quite a lot of playing, with mock fights and chasing around, especially among the youngsters.

MAN'S BEST FRIEND

It is because of the very fabric of wolf pack organization that dogs have become man's best friend. They have no great difficulty in adjusting to human society. When you acquire a puppy, your family becomes his pack and he will go through every stage of being a cub, just as he would have in the wild. He will try to gain status in the family, which is why timid people have problems with big powerful dogs. The dog simply wants to be the pack leader in matters that concern him. A timid dog just wants to lead a quiet life and he looks to you, his leader, to protect him and provide for him.

DOGS ARE DOGS

One of the major problems with humans is they have a tendency to apply human thoughts and traits to other animal groups, dogs included. It is true that dogs do have many of our emotions—love, hate, jealousy, happiness, and sadness—but they do not think like us. They do not apply reason to anything, but take things as they happen. If you try to think in terms of the way the wolf pack is organized then you will end up with a very obedient and happy dog. You must commu-

Because of their instinct to be part of a pack, dogs long ago adapted to living with human families, and we gladly took them in.

nicate to him in a manner that he can relate to, a manner that is basic to his species and not to yours. If you can grasp this point, then you are well on your way to success.

SOCIALIZATION AND HOUSETRAINING

Your dog begins learning from the minute he is born. By the time his eyes open, his mind has already been conditioned to more than you might think. His scenting ability is probably the first instinct to be used and this can affect his disposition. For example, if his mother is agitated at the approach of a certain human, then the puppy will scent this. A negative impression will be recorded in his mind and he may always be rather shy of humans. If the initial human contact is good, the puppy will grow up to have a strong liking for people.

Once his eyes open, the whole process of learning begins to accelerate and the environment starts to register in his mind. As he begins to scramble around, his brain receives many impulses. A vacuum cleaner may frighten him and become embedded in his memory as a negative experience. By the time you obtain the puppy at maybe 10 to 12 weeks of age, he has already formed a number of thoughts about his world, some good and some not so good. This is why some puppies seem very outgoing and fearless and others are timid and lack confidence. Of course, these factors are also influenced by the pup's genetic makeup, so the question of character is a complex matter.

THE INITIAL TRAINING

When you obtain your dog, he must be socialized into your family. Before you can

even think about training, the puppy must develop a bond with you. At this early age, he is very dependent on you for everything, so you quickly become his leader without having to enforce any form of discipline.

Your puppy must learn to understand his name. Simply repeating it over and over for a few days will achieve this. Each time you call the puppy to you, he will come running. He should be praised once he gets to you. An important lesson is being taught by praising him. He learns that coming to you is a pleasurable act that results in a lot of fuss. It is one of the most important lessons your dog will ever learn. When your dog comes to you he should

always be praised, never scolded or disciplined. If you observe this golden rule, your dog will always come to you with his tail wagging.

HOUSETRAINING

During the first week or two, the puppy should not be given unrestricted movement around your home. This has two benefits: it reduces the risk of him urinating or defecating in rooms with carpets, and it gets him used to the idea that he must stay where you put him. A puppy playpen or a dog crate will keep the puppy out of harm's way and restrict the area in which he can eliminate. It's not a good idea to keep the puppy secured to something with a collar and lead when

The more friendly strangers your puppy meets early on—human, canine and otherwise—the more secure and well adjusted he will feel as he grows up.

you are out of the room, as he can get tangled up and hurt himself or become afraid of the lead.

It's best to keep the puppy in the kitchen or in an enclosed patio during his housetraining period, assuming that the area is warm and free of drafts. A tile floor is the least inviting surface for a pup to eliminate on.

A puppy cannot regulate his bowels at all. This ability only comes at about four months of age, and even then not completely. On average, he will want to relieve himself about six times a day: in the morning when he wakes up, after his breakfast, around lunch time, in the afternoon, and probably twice during the evening before going to sleep. He will also want to relieve himself after playing or becoming excited. Most of his elimination will be urination.

Think of a crate as a special den for your puppy, where he will be undisturbed and out of harm's way until you can be with him.

Wire and fiberglass are the two most popular kinds of crate, and this Welsh Springer Spaniel puppy is getting out of his fiberglass one. Whichever you choose should be roomy enough for the dog to sit, stand, and lie down inside.

When the puppy wants to relieve himself, you must recognize the signs. He will whimper and run around searching for a suitable place, generally toward the walls of the room in a quiet spot. He prefers a soft surface (such as a carpet) to linoleum or tile. There are several methods of training the puppy.

Dirt Box

Use a large cat litter tray or a similar box with low sides, with a thin layer of garden soil in it. The soil should have previously been sifted and dried out. You can also line the box with newspaper. The minute you see the puppy searching for a spot to relieve himself, place him in the dirt box and gently hold him for a few seconds. He should then urinate. If he does not, and he jumps out of the box and

searches again, repeat the sequence and he will quickly get the message. After he is finished, give him lots of praise.

Once the puppy has full protection against distemper, hepatitis, and parvo, he should be taken outdoors regularly to a spot of dirt in the yard. The pup will quickly use the spot because there is no change in surface.

If you miss the puppy's signs that he is about to eliminate, he may have an "accident" on the floor. It is your responsibility to watch the pup at obvious times and get him to the dirt box. If a trained puppy or adult dog eliminates inside the home because he is not taken outside in time, it is the owner's fault. Once you start taking the pup outside, you must stay with it—rain, hail, or snow. If you don't, you will not know if he has relieved

Because accidents do happen it's important to have a stain and odor remover on hand. Stain Stealer removes new and old pet stains virtually on contact, and is completely safe for use around children, pets and plants. Photo courtesy of Francodex.

These Doberman puppies are confined to a bathroom where they have newspaper to relieve themselves on while they're in the early stages of housetraining. If they're not given a chance to make mistakes and are praised when they go in the right place, they will be housebroken in no time.

Make the crate a cozy place for your puppy by lining it with soft old sheets or blankets and leaving him a couple of toys to play with. (Golden Retriever)

on a schedule. Buy a crate that your puppy will be comfortable in as an adult, and until he is full grown, divide the crate so that the pup fits comfortably in a smaller section. Make the crate appealing by lining it with an old soft towel or blanket. Incorporate leaving the pup in his crate into his schedule for feeding, playing, etc., so that he will become accustomed to the crate as part of his daily routine. For example, take him out first thing in the morning. Praise him for eliminating outside. Bring him inside and feed him. He'll need to go out again about 15 minutes after breakfast. Let

A good diet makes housetraining easier because the higher the digestibility, the less waste products there are. A high-quality food will contain ingredients your puppy's body will use up fast. Photo courtesy of Nature's Recipe Pet Foods.

himself. The key to success is being observant and, during training, ensuring that the box is kept clean—a dog will not want to use a dirty "toilet."

Newspaper

You can spread a few sheets of newspaper on the floor and put the puppy on them when you see that he wants to relieve himself. Once he is using these without any problems, simply remove a few sheets so that only one sheet is left. Put the papers near a door that leads outside. Once you start taking the puppy outside, you can remove the paper and leave it down only at night. You must

be sure that the pup is taken outside regularly during the day.

Once the pup is a little older, he will be able to control his bowels overnight. If you see him relieve himself last thing at night, the paper can be removed altogether. Do not admonish the dog for relieving himself where the paper used to be—you used to praise him for doing his duty in that spot.

Crate

Crates are excellent aids to housebreaking because puppies and dogs do not want to eliminate where they sleep, and they help keep puppies him out to eliminate, play with him, and then put him in his crate. About an hour later, take him out of the crate and bring him outside. Praise him when he eliminates. If you keep to a schedule, which you must, toilet training will normally take only two weeks or so, assuming that the pup is old enough to be taken outside.

BEING LEFT ALONE

You should teach the puppy from a young age that he must become used to being left alone. At night, the puppy should be left in the kitchen (or in his crate) with a dog chew and maybe a cuddly toy. It will also help with a young pup if you place a clock with a loud tick near to the crate to simulate the heart-beat of his mother.

The puppy must be kept warm. The cuddly toy gives him something to snuggle up to. If he starts to cry, you must give him a while to see if he will settle down after realizing you are not coming. If he persists in crying or howling, then you must go to him and say "no" or "quiet." Do not pick him up, just say the word in a firm voice. Leave the room and repeat the sequence a few times if needed, raising your voice each time.

It should not take more than two or three nights to train the puppy to sleep quietly on his own, providing you do not give in to the temptation to cuddle him. This will merely convince him that if he persists enough, you will give in.

During the first few days it will be useful if you can leave the puppy for short periods in the kitchen by himself. If he starts to bark or howl, leave him alone and see if he quiets down. If not, simply repeat the sequence you use at night. If you have a persistent howler, you must take the matter to the next level. This means holding the pup with one hand and giving him a quick, *gentle* spank while firmly telling him "quiet" or "no." The object is to make the puppy realize that howling will be followed by a firm reprimand.

If all has gone well, you will have a clean and quiet puppy within about two to four weeks. Punishment during this initial socialization period should really be non-existent, or, at the very most, limited to a few little spanks. Whenever he does something that you do not want him to do, you must catch him in the act and say "no" in a firm voice. For a puppy this is usually quite sufficient, and it may be enough discipline even as he gets older.

Your puppy can enjoy hours of fun with a Nylafloss®. It's a great tug toy (when you initiate and end the game!), your puppy can retrieve it, and it does wonders for his dental health by massaging his gums and literally flossing between his teeth, loosening plaque and tartar build-up. Unlike cotton knot toys, Nylafloss® is made with the strongest, safest fibers (inert nylon), which won't rot or fray. The medium size is perfect for a puppy, like this Boston Terrier. Available at your local pet shop.

This Cocker Spaniel, Yankee Doodle's Dynamo, CDX, CGC, has perfected the heel on lead for his owner and has earned both the Companion Dog Excellent and Canine Good Citizen titles to boast of. Here he competes in a veteran's obedience class.

BEGINNING TO TRAIN YOUR DOG

Your dog will draw from his memory in order to decide on a course of action. His memory will tell him whether certain actions are pleasurable or not. This is the basis of training.

You know that your dog cannot understand your language, but that he can associate given sounds and their tones with given situations. If the sounds are also used in conjunction with hand signals, your dog can likewise link these to actions.

What a dog cannot do is relate to a time lapse situation. You cannot scold your dog for something he did in the past, nor can you tell him to do something in the future. The only thing your dog understands is the present because he lives from one moment to the next. This is *extremely* important for you to appreciate. If you do not understand this, you will get rather annoyed when things go wrong.

Here is a classic example: Your dog has run away from you and does not return when you call him. Eventually he does come, so you proceed to scold him and maybe give him a spanking. You are relating to an event that happened minutes before, but you are using human thinking. The dog relates to the moment. He associates coming back to you with being shouted at and spanked. When this happens again, which it will, the dog becomes confused.

He wants to come to you because you are his leader, but his memory reminds him that doing so may result in a spanking. The result is that he comes, but only half-heartedly. He wags his tail but crouches in submission, showing his confused state. He is trying to please you, yet he is not sure whether he will be praised or punished.

"But," you may say, "the dog must be punished, so how can I react differently?" Simple—you must *catch the dog in the act.* If you cannot, then no punishment is in order. You have to communicate at a level that the dog can understand, not at a level that you can, which is not always easy.

TRAINING SESSIONS

The length of time you should devote to training sessions will depend on a number of factors. If your dog is a puppy, or if he is an adult that has received little or no prior training, then sessions must be short. The puppy, like all infants, is not able to

concentrate on anything for very long. If you extend training sessions beyond his range of concentration, you will simply turn the pup off of training altogether.

Sessions should last for no more than about 20 minutes,

Even young puppies can learn basic commands if the lessons are short and rewarding. This Australian Cattle Dog pup "stands" for a treat.

and there should only be two sessions per day for the first few weeks. As the puppy gets older, you can increase the duration of the sessions. Also remember that if your dog is having a bad day, cancel the lessons. Like us, dogs have their off days and nothing is gained by trying to teach the

Puppy kindergarten is a great place to take your pup to meet other puppies and to give him his first obedience lessons.

When training, especially for advanced work like retrieving with a dumbbell, which this Rottweiler is doing, make sure you are in a quiet place where you have the dog's full attention.

dog when his mind just is not working as well.

All formal training sessions should begin with a short period of play. This puts the dog in a positive frame of mind. Next, you should start with an exercise that the dog already knows well. This will make the dog concentrate on the matter at hand, without him having to apply undue effort. The training session will then follow, and it must be ended on a positive note. Never risk boring the dog—once he has achieved the task of the day two or three times, stop. End each session with a little more play time.

You can teach your dog two or more commands at a time, but you must not proceed on to more advanced work until the basics have been mastered. What is also important is that you do not attempt to teach a puppy what might be termed "adult things" before he is old enough to cope with them. This will be crucial to all future training. Some trainers do not start advanced work until a dog is a least one year old.

Training sessions should be conducted in as much solitude as possible. You need the puppy's, or the dog's, full concentration. This will not be possible if other people are nearby or if the dog can see cars and dogs passing. An enclosed area, maybe a garage, will be fine for the first basic lessons. After that, you can go elsewhere, such as your local park, and find a quiet spot. Do not begin a training session just after your dog has eaten. This is especially important because he will generally feel sleepy and will want to relieve himself after a meal, both of which detract from his concentration.

TRAINING EQUIPMENT

There is a wide variety of dog training equipment available that is useful for everything from basic "manners" training to advanced obedience work. Some of the equipment is more specialized than the average dog owner really needs, so your selection should be based on the type of training you will be doing with your dog.

The yellow dummy this Irish Water Spaniel brings in is an example of a specialized piece of training equipment.

CHOKE COLLARS

The regular leather collar is not a good dog training aid in that its pressure on the dog's neck is constant. In order to be fully effective, the collar has to be tight enough so that the dog cannot slip out of it. It also needs to be able to be tightened and loosened quickly so that the dog feels variable pressure from the collar. The choke collar is thus the preferred choice for training. There are many forms of chokes, some better than others, and some more intimidating than others. All work on the principle that if a dog pulls forward or backward, the collar gets tighter, thus choking the dog. As the dog takes up the required position in relation to the handler, the choke eases. The advantage of the choke is that when the dog walks nicely by your side, there is no restriction at all on his neck. It is thus far more comfortable for the dog than a regular fixed-position buckle collar.

There are two types of choke collar. One is a single length of choke with a ring at each end. This is a single choke. The other consists of a single choke that is passed through another choke. As the second choke tightens, it forces the two rings of the first choke (the one around the dog's neck) together. This is a double choke. The double choke is limited because once the rings at each end of the choke on the dog's neck are brought together, no further choking is possible. With a single choke, the pressure increases in relation to the amount of pulling the dog does.

The Hercules™ Bone is made of very tough polyurethane and is designed for dogs that are strong chewers.

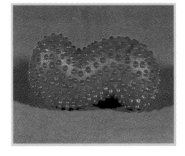

A choke chain is called such because it can be pulled up to tighten around a dog's neck— letting him know when he needs to pay special attention—or released to lay loose.

The prong-type choke is another variation. It is a double choke with metal stubs, or prongs, facing in toward the dog's neck. If the dog pulls, he feels the prongs, which are more painful than the regular choke. If the dog doesn't pull, he doesn't get poked by the prongs. Many people do not like how this collar looks and it is not allowed in obedience rings. However, it is more effective because the dog learns not to pull more quickly than with a regular choke. It should not be confused with earlier prong collars, which were single action and very painful.

Chokes may seem harsh, but they are really far more gentle in the long run than a regular collar. It is only a bad piece of equipment if the person controlling it makes it bad.

Chokes are available in metal, leather, and nylon, with metal being the preferred choice. Be sure, however, that the links of a metal choke are welded and not soldered. Soldered links are cheaper and less reliable where strong dogs are concerned, as a link may snap open. Choose reasonably large rings for a large breed, as they will not mark the coat as badly as small ones. Be sure that the links allow for very smooth action so they release pressure instantly when the dog eases back.

Chokes come in a wide range of lengths and sizes, so be sure you get the correct one. It should fit comfortably over the dog's head and rest on the back of his neck. It should not ride up to the dog's ears when under pressure, nor should it hang loose when the dog is at your side. To fit a single choke, feed the links through on one of the rings until they are all through. Pass the choke over the dog's head so that the ring snapped to the lead is such that its links are on the back of the dog's neck, not at the side. This will allow the choke to work smoothly. If you put it on the wrong way, the choke will not release properly as the dog eases back.

Remember that a choke collar is a training aid and not a regular collar. It must *never* be left on the dog when you are not present. Every year a number of dogs are choked to death when they get their collars caught on something and try to wriggle free.

LEADS

There are many types of leads, made from many types of materials. For training, you will need one that is about 5 or 6 feet long, and one that is much longer, up to 40 feet long, if you plan to train your dog for tracking or gun work. The best material for the long lead, or check line, is webbing, as nylon may burn your hand when you let the dog take up its length; it also tangles more easily. Either nylon or leather is preferable for your regular lead. Choose good quality every time—it will

A six-foot leather lead and a standard choke chain are all the equipment you need to teach basic commands. This Golden Retriever is being asked to "down" with a hand signal.

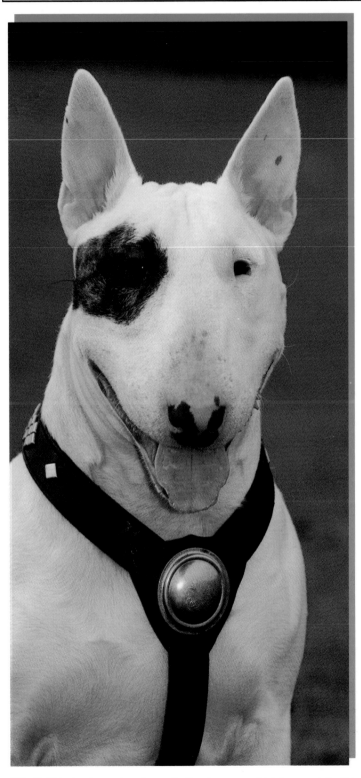

This Bull Terrier dons a handsome leather harness, which he wears for the special activities of tracking or weight pulling.

last longer. Leather leads should be double stitched and have a strong billet, or trigger type, fastening that won't suddenly bend open if the dog pulls hard. The lead must be supple so you can easily fold it up and put it in your pocket. A slip lead is like an enormous choke with a handle on the end. It has the same action as a choke and is available in either single or double. For training, I think that a choke collar is the better option. If you own a large breed, you may be tempted to purchase a short lead. While these are fine once your dog is trained, they are of no use initially.

You must choose a width that is appropriate for your breed. Whether or not you prefer a round or flat lead is up to you, but the flat lead is easier to hold if the dog is large and strong.

OTHER EQUIPMENT

The proper collar and a strong lead are essential for training your dog to heel, as well as to sit, down, come, and stay. Another extremely helpful piece of equipment is the dog crate. The crate will make housetraining a breeze, and it will also serve as a place to keep your dog safe and secure when you have company over and when you are not at home.

If you do get the training bug and you want to do the advanced work necessary to compete in hunting, herding, obedience trials, etc., you will need specialized equipment. This includes dumbbells for obedience, a harness for tracking, whistles and dummies for hunting, and so on. For the average owner, the proper collar, lead, and crate are all that will be necessary.

Every dog should learn these five basic commands: sit, stay, down, come, and heel. This Pointer sits for his owner while awaiting his next command.

THE BASIC COMMANDS

Sit, stay, heel, and down are commands that are basic to all training and that every dog should learn. These commands are fundamental to all further obedience training and will be needed time and again. If your dog has an understanding of these commands, combined with a full understanding of the word "no" and the willingness to respond to his name when called, he will be a well-mannered dog.

Each of these commands can be taught to a young puppy from about the age of 10 weeks. The puppy's ability to learn really starts around 10 to 16 weeks. Before this age, you can concentrate on beginning the pup's understanding of "no" and building a bond with him so he will happily come when called.

The sit and stay commands can be taught on a casual basis over a two-week period; no specific training sessions are needed. Give the puppy a few days to settle into his new home before introducing these commands.

Remember, words are merely sounds to your dog and he will link them to expected actions. Do not confuse your dog with a discourse, simply state what you want him to do in the simplest way you can. If he does as requested, he gets lots of praise. If he does not, the command is repeated and he receives whatever discipline is needed to con-

vince him that obeying is the more pleasurable option.

NO

Every dog must fully understand the most basic

Your puppy will test you in all sorts of ways, and "no" should be a part of his vocabulary so he knows when he's done wrong. This Golden pup is going for a plate of nachos.

command of all—the word "no." It is a command you will use a great deal, especially with a puppy. You can use it from the first day you obtain the pup, but of course only in a gentle voice and only at the moment of a misdemeanor.

If he starts to chew on a slipper, you should approach him quietly, take hold of the slipper, and say "no" in a firm voice. No other action is needed. If he keeps chewing,

repeat the sequence. The object is simply to put into the puppy's mind that chewing on a slipper, which is a pleasurable act, results in you becoming annoyed, which is a non-pleasurable act. The pup must reach the point where the unpleasantness of your reaction is greater than the pleasure of chewing.

From the outset, you should determine the things that you do not want your dog to do and be very consistent in making sure that he does not do them. If you give a puppy an old slipper to play with, you cannot get annoyed when he chews your new ones. Slippers and shoes, old or new, are all the same to a dog, who places no value on material things. If the puppy jumps up on a chair you do not want him to go on, lift him off and say "no." You must, however, do this on every single occasion. If you are inconsistent, the puppy will detect that your resolve is weak and will not consider "no" to be the emphatic instruction that it should be.

As with all commands, there can be no question of the dog not obeying, so unless you fully intend to enforce a command, don't give it in the first place. Be aware also that obeying commands does not necessarily pertain to the whole family. Just because the dog will obey you does not mean that he will obey anyone else! He probably will, but a strong-willed dog may challenge each member of the family to see which of them he can ignore in given situations. Dogs are very intelligent and will soon be trying to see how they can circumnavigate your commands!

If a puppy habitually disobeys a "no" command, you are not getting the message across. For example, the pup continues to play with the slipper even though you have told him "no." Approach the pup quietly, take hold of the slipper, and say "no" in a very firm voice. At the same time, give the pup a slap on the nose or on the backside. He should then associate the "no" with a displeasing feeling and refrain from doing anything when you say no.

Remember that the compulsion to do certain things will vary with the dog's thresholds. He is therefore far more likely to disobey a "no" command in certain situations than in others. Chasing a cat is a low-threshold instinct. Saying "no" in the same voice that you use when the puppy is chewing a slipper will probably not be sufficient to override his instinct to chase a cat; a much firmer tone of voice will be needed.

If you do your homework, your puppy should react pretty quickly to a "no" command in most instances. He should not progress to doing things that will later require a more severe form of punishment. Inappropriate behaviors can be prevented only if the

owner instills in the puppy that when he says "no," he really means it, and that to disobey will result in a negative experience *every single time.*

The "no" command has many applications to the puppy and is the first command the pup will learn that can be applied at long range. As with all aspects of training, the name of the game is to get your message across with the minimum of discipline. However, if you fail to teach your dog the "no" command to an extent that he fully understands it, then I regret to say that you will certainly be forced into the situation where your dog is going to have to endure much harder discipline down the line. Try to get things right while the pup is still a pup!

The command "stand" comes in handy when you want to groom your dog, or when the veterinarian needs to examine him.

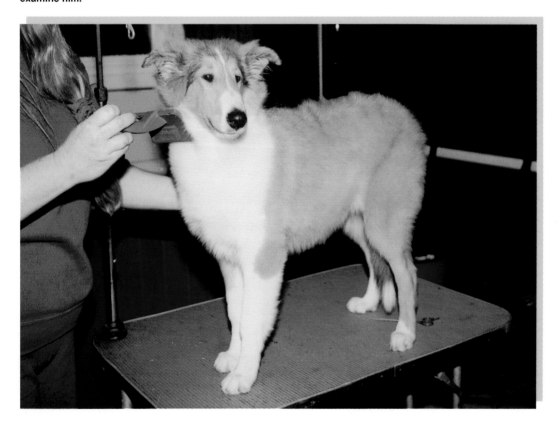

Teach your puppy that "sit" means to plant his hindquarters on the ground. Praise him when he does it right.

SIT

The sit is easily taught and can normally be learned in a few short informal sessions. With the puppy next to you, tell him to sit while pushing down on his hindquarters with one hand and placing the other hand gently under his chin or on the top of his chest. He will have no option but to sit. Give him lots of praise and repeat the sequence. Twice is enough to start with. You can give the puppy one or two more lessons at intervals throughout the day and over the next couple of days. Remember, keep it simple, just say "sit." If the puppy should roll over, gently pick him back up and start again.

STAY

This command is also easily learned and is a natural follow-up to the sit. Start by having the dog sit once or twice so his mind is focused on what he is doing. Call the puppy to you and have him sit in front of you. Once he is sitting, tell him to "stay." He will probably get up and come to you. Lift him up and put him back in the original spot. Push his bottom down and tell him to sit, then say "stay" and move back a little. If the pup holds the stay for a few seconds, you can praise him. If he persists in getting up without staying at all, you must be even more persistent until he does as he is told.

As the pup catches on to the command, you can move back a few feet. As you give the command, hold up your right

This Golden pup is responding properly to "down" and "stay" for his happy owner.

hand, showing your palm to the pup. Once he masters this, you can move further away, perhaps about 20 feet away from the pup. Give the hand

Neva Sharlow keeps Joslyn's attention on her while teaching the heel by holding a tennis ball in her left hand. This keeps Joslyn interested in being right by her side.

signal along with the verbal command. You should not expect a young puppy to remain sitting for very long, so just concentrate on having him stay for about ten seconds at a time. Of course, the puppy should receive lots of praise for every successful stay.

Providing you are persistent, the sit and stay will be accom-

Make training enjoyable by rewarding your dog with a nutritional chew like the Carrot Bone™ from Nylabone®. It contains no plastics or artificial ingredients of any kind, so it's a 100%-natural plaque, obesity and boredom fighter. Available at your local pet shop.

Start slow with leash training and your dog, like these Welsh Springer Spaniels, should never mind walking on lead with you.

Wil de Veer's Am Staff puppy starts out on a lightweight nylon lead. No problem!

plished in no time at all. Remember, the sit must be in the same spot—the pup must not move. Keep your lessons short with play periods before and after, and always end with something the pup knows how to do.

WALK ON LEAD AND HEEL

Before the puppy can be taught to heel, he must first become familiar with his collar and lead. You can collar-train the puppy as soon as you bring him home. Put his collar on and leave it on for a few hours each day—within a day or two he will think nothing of it. You can clip the lead onto the collar and just let the puppy pull it along. He will get used to the feel of the lead's weight. Leave it on for a little while at a time, perhaps two or three times a day. It should only take about two days for him to become accustomed to it.

The next step is to hold the lead and let the puppy wander about. Every now and then, give the lead a little tug while calling the puppy to you and praising him for coming. Some trainers believe in teaching the pup very quickly by walking with him on the lead and dragging him if necessary. However, it's best to take your

time in accustoming the pup to walking on a lead without dragging the puppy around the floor. You should try to achieve everything in the gentlest manner at first.

Once the pup's inoculations have taken full effect, you can commence more formal training in the garage or another quiet location. Around 12 to14 weeks is the right age for heel work.

Try to have the puppy near a wall so that he does not have unlimited space to move to his left (or to his right if you are left handed). You can now place the choke chain, nylon choke, or slip lead on the puppy. The puppy will be eager to explore and will probably want to run off ahead of you. If he sits down and does not want to budge, then coax him to you and fuss over him. Soon he will overcome his fear of the new situation and start walking.

You must hold the lead correctly. You will hold it in your right hand and pass it through your left (or reverse if left-handed), which will be the hand that actually controls

the dog. With a small dog, you can hold the lead in your left hand at about waist level, at the middle of your body. When the puppy starts to pull ahead of you, give the lead a sharp tug with your left hand while saying "heel" in a quiet but firm voice. Continue walking, and if the pup starts to get ahead again, repeat the action.

If you have no wall to walk against, chances are that the puppy will begin moving to your left as well as ahead of you. To correct this, pull both

When training is paired with a treat—especially in the form of a POPpup™— your dog will be eager to learn. POPpups™ contain no plastics and no preservatives, just 100% goodness in a chew that can be given as is or microwaved to a biscuit consistency.

backward and toward you at the same time. This will no doubt spin the puppy in his tracks, but it won't take many such pulls to convince him that he is better off close to your side. Once he is in the required position, praise him. Keep the first lesson short and be sure to end on a positive note, with the dog near your side. At this stage you are not looking for perfection—a little progress in each session is quite enough.

It will not take many sessions to have your dog walking nicely by your side. He should walk so that his shoulders are approximately level with your left knee. It will certainly help matters if you ensure that the pup stays focused on the matter at hand.

Sudden changes in direction will help solve certain problems. For example, an about-turn will just about pull the puppy off of his feet; however, it will help cure him of pulling ahead. Likewise, if you make a sudden right turn, the pup will be somewhat shaken up but he will begin to concentrate on watching your movements. When you make a left turn, chances are that you will walk straight into the pup with your left leg. Do not flinch from doing this, as a few bumps from your leg will teach him to be mindful of your whereabouts. However, be a little more careful with a small dog, because if you should tread on his toes he will become frightened of being near you.

How precise you are in heel work with your dog is a matter of individual preference. If you plan to enter obedience competitions, you will need to train your dog to a high standard of perfection. If you just want a

A precise heel takes a lot of practice, on lead and off. Here a Chesapeake Bay Retriever heels on lead during a figure eight exercise in Novice obedience.

well-behaved dog, precision is not required. For normal walking, you simply want the dog to be in a good heel position.

One common problem is the tendency for the dog to move out too far to the left. This can be dangerous because someone could trip over the lead if they are coming the other way. Any tendency of the pup to move too far from you must be corrected by giving a quick jerk toward you, combined with patting your knee and giving the heel command.

Heel and Sit

The heel and sit commands are used together when you come to a standstill. As you stop walking, tell the dog to sit. If he does not, simply use your left hand to push his rear end down while holding the lead up with your right hand so that the dog's head is lifted and he is encouraged to sit. If you have already taught the puppy to sit, this will not be a problem. Repeated a few times, your dog will automatically sit once you come to a standstill. If he does not, simply tell him to sit.

Once you have the dog doing the heel and sit, you can try varying the pace of your walk. The most difficult for dogs is a slow walk, as they tend to want to get to wherever you are going. On a fast walk, watch that the dog does not suddenly try to run. When you are running, be sure that the dog keeps pace with you rather than shooting in front of you. This will need much practice if you think it is worth the effort.

Heel Off Lead

Once your dog can heel and sit correctly, you can try the exercise without the lead. If the dog starts to wander or move ahead in spite of your command to heel, put him back on the lead—he clearly has not learned the command well enough yet. One way to overcome problems is to attach a very fine but strong cord to the dog's collar. Unclip the lead and tell the dog to heel. He knows he is off lead, but might not realize that he is still under your control. As he starts to move ahead, give a sudden hard jerk and say "heel"—he will be surprised. After this, he will not be sure if he is on some form of lead or not, and he should perform better. In all training, you should always try to be one move ahead of the dog.

No matter how well-trained your dog is, he should always be on a lead where there is traffic. There is always the risk of him becoming spooked or forgetting all of his training and running out into the road. Don't ever chance it.

A puppy can be enticed into the down position by following a treat you hold in your hand.

Staying in the down position is a lot more enjoyable when there's something to chew on. A stick will do, but a Nylabone® is safer and healthier!

Down

This command is necessary if you plan to enter obedience competitions, but is of no real value if you own a pet dog. Your dog will automatically lie down if this is more comfortable than sitting, and there is no valid reason to make him sit if he is happier lying down.

Some dogs, especially strong-willed ones, may have trouble accepting this command, as it is an act of submission in their eyes. Until they understand that it is not your intention to punish them, they are likely to be stubborn about obeying this order. There are a few ways to train a dog to go into the down position.

With your dog sitting in front of you, hold the lead with your right hand. As you give the down command, pull the dog down and hold him for a second or two, praising the dog when he is in position. Repeat this a few times until the dog gets the message.

Another on-lead method is to place your left foot over the lead so that it passes under the space between the heel and the sole. Hold the lead in your right hand and stand at right angles

to the dog. On the command "down," pull the lead up high while pressing the dog's shoulders with your left hand. Once down, praise the dog and ease back on the lead. If he tries to get up, put him back into position with the lead, again saying "down" and praising the dog once he is in position. This method is most intimidating to the dog, and he will probably wriggle backwards in protest.

Another method is to kneel in front of your dog, grasp his two front elbows, and bring them gently but swiftly forward. The dog has no option but to go down. Quickly release your left hand and place it on the dog's shoulders while praising the dog. If his size permits, you can secure both of his front feet on the floor with your right hand. The alternative method, using the same principle, is to hold the dog's collar in your left hand and bring your right hand up behind the dog's legs so he goes down. Place your weight (only sufficient to achieve the objective) on the dog's shoulders to hold him in place for a few seconds. With either method, repeat the sequence a few times, giving lots of praise once the dog is in the down position. You may need two or three lessons before the dog understands what is expected.

The basic commands must be practiced until the dog responds promptly to them. It is not enough that they are done, they must be done correctly and quickly. This means plenty of practice and much patience on your part. Once you have taught your dog these commands, he is well on his way to becoming a polite and well-mannered canine.

ADVANCED BASIC COMMANDS

If you have succeeded with basic commands, you may wish to build on them and do more advanced work with your dog. If you really get hooked on training your dog, advanced commands will enable you to enter obedience trials and work toward earning obedience titles on your dog.

SIT /STAY

Bring the pup to the heel and sit position on the lead. If your pup is already proficient at staying on command, you can let the lead trail over his shoulder. If not, you must hold on to the lead. The hand signal for a stay from this position is to hold your arm down with the palm facing the dog's head and just in front of his nose. Say "stay," walk a few paces forward, and turn to face the dog. Initially, if the dog obeys the command, you should only expect him to stay for about 15 to 20 seconds. Then you can return and take your position next to him, giving him a lot of praise.

If the dog attempts to move toward you after you have given the command, you must simply take the dog back to his original spot and repeat the command. Practice this until the dog sits straight and does not attempt to move from his spot. Ultimately, you want the dog to stay in position for one minute if he is to compete in the Novice obedience class, so be sure he will stay for a little longer than this just to be on the safe side.

It is important that the dog does not attempt to move once he sees you returning to him. If he does, you know the drill—back to his original spot and walk away to complete the exercise. You will need lots of patience in teaching the long stay to your dog, so never lose your temper and start yelling at him. Just use a progressively firmer "stay."

LONG DOWN

For Novice obedience tests, your dog will need to stay in the down position for three minutes. Since he understands the stay command by now, the down/stay should be easy. Some dogs have the tendency to sit up when you return to the heel position, so make sure he is trained to stay in the down position until you say otherwise. Don't forget that training is more

Jerry and Linda Grzywacz's Golden, Empyreal Perfect Strike, strikes the perfect pose as he enjoys a sunny day in the garden.

The figure eight exercise reminds your dog that he should stay by your side while walking among other people. This Golden gets the idea.

about praise than discipline, so be extra generous with praise every time your dog performs as he should. He's obeying you so he can be fussed over!

RECALL

In the recall test, you must heel and sit the dog, then tell him to stay. You will walk a given distance from him and turn to face him. After he has stayed in position for a given amount of time, you will call the dog to you.

To teach this command, keep the dog on the lead and walk away, holding the lead. Turn to face the dog and, when ready, call him to you. You may say "come" or simply his name, or both—"Fido, come." If it helps your dog to concentrate, then by all means use his name each time.

When the dog comes on a recall, he should stop straight in front of you in the sit position and look at you. He should be close enough that if

he had something in his mouth he could give it to you without your having to unduly stretch. Repeat the exercise until your dog is doing it well. He should not sit sloppily or sideways, but straight ahead of you—in competition this is usually an important factor. If you do not plan to compete with your dog then obviously it need not be so precise, but it should still be good.

FINISH

The finish is the term given to a dog going from the sit position to the heel after a recall. First, have the dog in the sit position in front of you on his lead. Clench the lead in your left hand, knuckles upward, and get a good grip on it. Tell the dog to heel, and at the same time step back with your left leg and jerk the dog toward you. Then, in one continuous movement, move your left leg back level with your right leg so you are in the original starting position. At the same time, relax your

hold on the lead, because by now the dog will have turned to his left and will be at your side. Tell him to sit and after a second or two, if he is in the correct position, give him a lot of praise. You will need to practice this a few times, but the dog will soon get the idea.

Another way to teach the finish is to have the dog go around the back of you into the heel and sit position. Take the lead in your right hand and tell the dog to heel. At the same time, step back and the dog will approach you on your right hand side. Once he or she is level with you, step forward and pass the lead over, behind your back, to your left hand. Stand still, and the dog will come alongside of you to complete the finish. I prefer this method because it involves no hard jerking on the lead, and the dog does not have to do a sudden about-turn. I also think it is a smarter looking finish.

FIGURE EIGHT

The object of the figure eight exercise is to have your dog at your side while making both right and left turns. In order to train him, you will need two poles, each about 3 feet high when staked into the ground. The poles will give your dog something to actually go around rather than just walk over. The distance between the poles is not important; about 10 feet is fine. Begin in the middle and proceed so that the first pole is taken to your right. Your dog will tend to go right, so encourage him to stay close to you by patting your left knee. On left turns the dog may try to push ahead or lag behind, both of which are undesirable.

Whether a Sporting breed like a Labrador Retriever or a Toy breed like this Shih Tzu, your dog should come right away—and happily—when called.

Do a number of circuits and, if all is going well, change the pace somewhat so that you go both faster and slower. Work on the figure eight until your dog is performing in a smooth manner. Do not forget to give him plenty of praise when you come to the end of the session. Once the dog is proficient on the lead, practice the exercise with the dog off lead.

STAND

This command is not as easily learned as the sit or down commands and requires a lot of repetition. When the dog is sitting next to you, give the stand command and at the same time lean over the dog and lift him so he is in the required position. Give him praise. You must not overdo the repetition, simply add it to his repertoire so it is learned over a number of training sessions. Always remember that any exercise repeated too many times will bore your dog. He will lose his concentration and this will tend to make you annoyed. It is far better that you take your time and keep sessions short. As your dog learns more, there will be more of a variety of exercises to go over, which will be more interesting. End each session with something your dog is good at so you can give him lots of praise.

STAND FOR EXAMINATION

This exercise is part of the Novice obedience test. Its object is to show that your dog is not aggressive with strangers. It is obviously best taught while a dog is young, before he has developed any negative attitudes toward strangers.

Using a hand signal, this trainer instructs his Weimaraner to stay while standing. Next, he will walk away from the dog for a little while to test him.

Practice enthusiastic recalls by running backwards while you call your dog to you. This will make him think you're running away, and he'll want to chase you. Praise him as he closes in on you.

Apart from being necessary at shows, this command has practical value for all dogs. When they go to the veterinarian, they will be less nervous if they are used to people touching them. They will be less likely to snap at strangers who try to pet them.

Have your dog in the heel and stand position and tell him to stay, using the palm of your hand to his nose as a hand signal. Move to the end of the training lead but be sure to keep it slack. Hold the dog in position for a few seconds and return by walking around the dog to come to the heel position. Stand there for a few seconds before ending the exercise. When your dog is familiar with this routine, you can have a friend walk up to the dog while the dog is still standing by your side. The friend should touch the dog's head and take his hand along the dog's back to touch the tail. If there are no problems, you can proceed to have your friend examine the dog while you face the dog at the end of the lead. Next, try the exercise while the dog is off lead and you are a few feet further back. The examiner should run his hands down the dog's hindquarters as well as over the dog's head, back, and tail.

ADVANCED STAY AND RECALL

By this stage in your dog's training, he should be very well-behaved. However, in order to perfect the basic training, you must see if you can increase the temptation for the dog to disobey a command. One way would be to enlist the help of others who have well-trained dogs. If you can enlist such help, have a number of handlers form a line and place their dogs in the heel and sit position. Next, all owners should give the stay command and walk away from their dogs. The dogs should be recalled, one at a time, by their owners.

The chances are good that as the first dog moves, so will one or two others. If yours is one of them, you should move toward him, take hold of his collar, and lead him straight back to his original position. Now, return to your previous place. Each of the other owners will do likewise. The whole process is repeated until all of the dogs have been recalled. Practice this until your dog will stay until you recall him. You will find that the exercise becomes progressively more difficult for your dog the longer he has to wait for the recall.

With advanced training, you should be able to use just your hands to let your dog know what you want her to do. It takes an enthusiastic pupil, like this Collie, and a patient trainer to learn the signals slowly but surely.

HAND SIGNALS

There are numerous benefits of having your dog understand hand signals. You may be at such a distance that the dog may not be able to hear your voice, or you may find occasions when it is more expedient to give a signal rather than a command. The working dog owner will find that he may not want to use his voice, which might startle game. In the obedience Utility class, dogs are tested on their ability to understand hand signals.

In order for signals to be effective, they must be very clear and not likely to be confused with any others. Also, they should be used every time the verbal commands are given so your dog will come to associate one with the other.

When your dog knows "sit" and "stay," you can pose him for pictures anywhere. This is Kreekside Basil, owned by Hans and Linda Koller.

HEEL

One of two signals may be used for the heel command. The first is with the hand directed downward and slightly away from the body, with the index finger pointing

This trainer uses her outstretched hand to communicate to her German Shepherd that she wants him to slow down as he nears the top of the teeter-totter in agility.

towards the ground. The other is with the hand pointed away from the body, but with the palm full face and toward the dog.

STAY

If the dog is in the heel position, you can use the outstretched arm at an angle with the face of the palm turned toward the dog. The open hand is what the dog will understand as the signal.

DOWN

Hold your hand high above your head and then bring it down to waist level in one sweeping movement. The arm can be outstretched or somewhat bent; it will be the downward swing that will the dog will react to. A signal used

by many obedience enthusiasts is to hold the arm at a right angle to the body with the arm bent upward from the elbow. The palm will face the dog so that the signal is similar to the signal a policeman uses to stop a vehicle. However, this could be confusing to the dog at a distance.

RECALL OR COME

The signal you use will depend on your dog's position. If the dog is relatively close to you, either ahead or behind, then the heel signal is, in effect, a come signal. If the dog is close, but in front of you, simply point your outstretched index finger to the floor in front of you to have the dog come to the frontal sit position. If the dog is at some distance from you, raise both hands above your head and clap. A single arm action is used in advanced obedience tests—raise your right arm above your head and bring it down to your left shoulder in one sweeping motion, with your palm facing your shoulder. The dog will associate the sweeping motion to the shoulder with the command.

DIRECTIONAL SIGNALS

These involve pointing your index finger in the direction you wish the dog to go. Start with your right arm in the bent position in front of your chest. In one fast action, point to your right with your arm extended slightly upward. This tells your dog to go to his left. The reverse, using your left arm, tells the dog to go to his right (remember, the dog is looking at you and will go in the direction opposite to the arm you are using). The same arm action and pointing finger are used to give your dog a line during directional retrieving. If practiced a great deal, the dog will come to associate the signal with a general direction and not just simply as a "go" command.

SIT FROM DOWN POSITION

If the dog is in the down position in front of you, he can be brought to the sit position by holding your hand, palm upward, at waist level. Next, raise the outstretched hand upwards. If the dog is in the sit position, you simply repeat the signal. Your dog will soon come to understand that the signal tells him to go to the next "up" position from the position he is in—from down to sit and from sit to stand.

SIT

One signal you can use is a raised finger with the thumb projected out. The hand

points to the dog and the rest of the fingers are clenched into the palm. If the dog is close to you, keep your hand close to your body at about waist level or just a bit higher. If the dog is at more of a distance, raise your arm higher.

WALK FROM THE HEEL POSITION

You should get into the habit of always moving off from the stationary position with your left leg. When your dog sees this, he will know that he must stand and start moving forward. When you do an about-turn, you will find it useful to do a quick one-two step to communicate your intentions to the dog.

REPETITION FOR SUCCESS

Your dog will tend to forget hand signals if they are not used on a regular basis. Once the dog understands the signals, chances are that you will tend to use them instead of verbal commands. You will also find that once the dog knows the hand signals well, you can keep your arm closer to your body than you did during training if the dog is working close to you. At a distance the signals should always be made very clear, because the farther away the dog is, the less he is able to focus.

In the Utility obedience classes, trainers have to instruct their dogs using only hand signals. Here a Cocker Spaniel is being asked to stay while his owner keeps walking.

SPECIALIZED TRAINING

RETRIEVING

It is very natural for a dog to retrieve an object. It embodies three basic instincts of the wild dog: the chase, the kill, and the return to the den with the spoils. All dogs have the instinct to retrieve, but during domestication it has become somewhat diluted in certain breeds. As a result, the degree of difficulty found in training a dog to bring back an object will vary not only from one breed to another, but also from one individual to another within a breed.

Your interest in serious retrieving work will either be in respect to obedience competition or related to field trials and hunting with gundogs. In either case, if you plan to train your dog to retrieve, he should not be encouraged to play with sticks or balls to any great degree while he is a puppy. Once a dog's training has begun, all items used for retrieves (specialized dumbbells or dummies) must be used for that purpose only, never as toys. If dogs start to play with sticks before they are trained, they may develop bad habits such as not returning to the owner with the object.

The best age to start training your dog to retrieve is four to six months old. Be sure that the dumbbell is the correct size and type for your breed. For working gundogs you will need canvas dummies or their equiva-

lent, which are sold at sporting shops.

Retrieving for Obedience

To begin training, find a location where there are no distractions. Begin by throwing the dumbbell into the air a few times to arouse your

In retriever hunting test and field trial training, handlers give their dogs a line on a bird before sending them to retrieve it.

dog's interest in the object. Next, you can pretend to throw the object, which will further arouse the dog's instinct to chase. Now you can throw the dumbbell, but not too far. This is to see if your dog will fetch it with enthusiasm. If he does, call the dog to you and have him sit in front of you holding the dumbbell. Take hold of the right end of the dumbbell and tell the dog to "leave it." Repeat the command with a

little more conviction if the dog does not give up the object, while tapping his nose lightly with your left hand. If the dog gives up the dumbbell easily, give him lots of praise and repeat the exercise.

In the first one or two sessions, only repeat the exercise three or four times to keep the dog's interest. Don't forget to throw the dumbbell in the air a few times before each retrieve so the dog retains his interest. If your dog learns quickly, begin throwing the dumbbell a little bit further on a progressive basis. Keep practicing until your dog always gives you a clean retrieve.

The next stage is to have the training lead on your dog and put him in the heel and sit position. Throw the dumbbell after telling the dog to stay. It is probable that he will go after the dumbbell the minute he sees it flying through the air—be ready for this. As he takes off, simply snap the lead back. Say nothing, but return the dog to the heel and sit position. If you have an extra long training lead, this will be more effective than a regular lead. You can always tie a length of rope to a regular lead to make it a good training lead.

With the dog back at your side and sitting steady, you can release the lead. He should maintain the sit position while you straighten up and he should not start wriggling to be free when he sees you about to release the lead. If this happens, just straighten up again and repeat the stay command (using the hand signal to his nose as well). Once he realizes what is required, you can issue the "fetch" or whatever command you have decided to use. The dumbbell should be returned to you and the dog should come close enough so that you can easily take it from him.

With practice, your dog should return to you and sit with the dumbbell until you take it from him. Initially, you should not make the dog wait more than a few seconds, and you can gradually increase the time.

A common problem is that the dog, having picked up the dumbbell, does not return right away and starts to play with it. This must be discouraged. The best way to do this is to start to run away from the dog when you see that he has the dumbbell in his mouth. His attention will be drawn to your departure, so he will forget about playing and come after you (hopefully, still holding onto the dumbbell!). Turn to face your dog when he comes near you, so you are ready to have him sit and give up the dumbbell. Give lots of praise and repeat a few times before ending on a high note.

Gundog Training

Working gundogs and tracking dogs must be able to retrieve an object correctly, present it to the owner, and not damage the object in any way. If a retriever chewed up a shot

In the field, the dumbbell is replaced by a bird, which the dog must find, retrieve, and deliver to his handler. This Brittany has learned his lessons well and delivers the bird with style.

bird, or one that was not dead, he would be a very poor retriever indeed. A dog that can return the object without marking it in any way is called soft-mouthed, while a dog that marks the object would be termed hard-mouthed.

It is because of mouthing that dumbbells are not recommended for working retriever breeds. By using canvas or equivalent soft dummies, you are able to determine the degree of pressure that the dog is using on the object. If such breeds are trained on hard objects, it tends to encourage a firmer grip, which is not good for retrieving gamebirds. Working retrievers must learn standard retrieves,

water retrieves, and blind retrieves. These all require highly specialized training.

JUMP TRAINING

Dogs enjoy jumping, but in order to enter obedience tests they need to be taught to jump in a regulated sequence. Your dog should be at least six months of age before you begin any form of jump training because the dog's front limb assembly is still developing up to this age and can be easily damaged when the dog lands on his front feet.

For the purposes of the Open obedience test your dog will need to be proficient in two types of jump: the high jump and the broad, or long, jump. If you join a training

class these will be provided by the instructor, but you should have your own so that your dog can practice at home.

The rules state that a dog should be able to clear a height of one-and-one-half times his height at the withers with a minimum of 12 inches and a maximum of 36 inches, though there are exceptions to this rule.

The First Jumps

If you are training a puppy (under nine months of age) to jump, you should not expect him to clear the same height as an adult. You will have to assess a suitable height for the pup. When you are ready to try the first jump, place one 8-inch board on the jump.

To teach the bar jump, which this Dalmatian clears with room to spare, you must start low and raise the bar gradually, praising every time the dog clears the jump. If you raise the bar too soon, your dog may duck under the bar instead, and you'll have to start over.

Smaller dogs get smaller jumps. A Papillon sailing over a broad jump shows that Toy breeds can do it, too—and love it!

You will be jumping this with your dog, who will be on his lead. Stand a few feet away from the jump and have your dog in the heel and sit position. When you move off, tell the dog to heel and go quickly over the jump. The dog will follow and should have no trouble clearing the jump. Practice this a few times and as you reach the jump say "over" or a similar command.

Next, you will increase the jump by one board, the size of which depends on your dog's size. Again, repeat the same steps. If you cannot jump this height yourself, go to one side and give enough slack on the lead so that the dog can take the jump. Do not forget to give your dog the verbal command as he reaches the jump. You should continue to practice with the dog on the lead. Do not make the jump too high too quickly; this will discourage the dog if he hits a board as he jumps.

By continued practice on the lead, the dog will build the confidence he needs to clear the boards every time. You can steadily add extra boards until you reach the maximum height for your dog's size. Should the dog falter at the last minute, he has not yet developed enough confidence at the previous level, so keep practicing.

At each height, you should have the dog do a return jump in the opposite direction. You can stay in the same position and change hands in holding the lead. Be sure that at all times there is enough slack in the lead, but not too much.

When you are confident that the dog can clear a given height, it can be tried without the lead. At the next height, place the lead back on. This way, the dog is always being given guidance and he will gain confidence. After each jump, your dog should take up the sit position in front of you, going to heel on command.

Bar Jumping

As your dog starts to improve in his high jumping over boards, you can teach him to bar jump. Train him the same way, but spend plenty of time at the lower heights. As the bar goes up, it increases the risk that the dog might decide to take the easier path—straight under the bar. Should the dog run under the bar, simply take him back and put his lead on. Lower the bar one or two pegs and perhaps place one or two solid boards in the jump so he cannot go under the bar. In both board and bar jumping, it is recommended that you train your dog to jump somewhat higher than will be required under test conditions.

Broad Jumping

Although it seems easy for a dog to negotiate a broad jump, the reality is quite the opposite. From the dog's viewpoint, the broad jump is not as

An Airedale makes the retrieve over the high jump look easy, but it wasn't until he had both his retrieving and his jumping down that his trainer combined the exercises.

easily gauged as the high jump, because the distance only becomes apparent when the dog is virtually on top of the first hurdle. Also, since the hurdles are not that high, the dog often steps between them or to the side of them.

You will initially have the dog on the lead. You should space the hurdles so there is not enough room between them for the dog to place his front feet. Start by using the lowest hurdles and space them a few inches apart. If your dog already does the high jump, you will not need to do the actual jumps yourself. You will run to the hurdles with the dog, but step to the side. Use the same verbal commands and procedures as with the high jump. On his first jump, the dog might land between hurdles. If this happens, reduce the distance and at the same time marginally increase the approach speed.

The timing of your verbal command is very important because in the early training it will help the dog gauge when to jump. Soon he will become so familiar with the jumps that he will come to know exactly when to take off. Once your dog jumps with ease *every* time and with inches to spare, you can proceed to the next stage. You will use a long training lead and place the dog a few feet from the jump, in the sit/stay position. You will stand at the end of the jump and call the dog, giving him the "over" command as he reaches the lift-off point. Turn your shoulder in the direction that the dog is traveling, as if you are about to start running. This will encourage the dog to put some effort into the jump.

Hitting the last bar on the broad jump means the dog didn't take off at the right time or wasn't ready for such a long distance. The proper verbal command and reducing the length will solve those problems.

Once your dog has mastered the broad jump on the lead, you can try it off lead. If he bypasses the jump, put the lead back on and keep practicing. It may help to place the jumps near a wall, which immediately eliminates one possible detour.

Jump and Retrieve

If retrieving and jumping are going well, you can combine the two. Start at a low height and work up progressively. The dog's ability to hold on to the dumbbell while performing another command will be tested. Once again, you will start with the dog on the lead and run up to the jumps with him. If the dog drops the dumbbell, you must correct him on the spot. Often it is just a case of the dog losing concentration as his mind fixes on the jump. After he has run a number of times with you, place the dog in the sit/stay position on his long training lead, with him holding the dumbbell. Go through the exercise a number of times from this position before you try it without the lead.

Don't be too discouraged if your dog drops the dumbbell a few times in the early sessions. Make due allowance for the dog to make mistakes and you will not become agitated. Just start again and keep practicing.

The final aspect of the jump and retrieve exercise entails your dog going for the dumbbell after you have thrown it over the jump. The dog must jump the high or broad jump in both directions and return to you as he would on a flat retrieve and recall. Be as good with the throw as you expect your dog to be in his jump and retrieve.

One problem is the tendency for the dog to return with the dumbbell around the side of the jump. If this happens, walk toward the jump and head the dog off. Take hold of his collar, return him to the spot where he picked up the dumbbell, and encourage him to make the return jump by patting the top of the jump. Return to your original position so that your dog can complete the exercise by sitting in front of you and finishing with a heel once you have taken the dumbbell.

In the jump and retrieve exercise, your dog may anticipate a command, a common problem in many exercises. The best way to discourage this is not to follow through with the usual command on every occasion. This will keep the dog guessing and at attention as he will be expecting a command, but he will not be sure that the expected command will be given every time. The dog will not work based on probability and will work only on actual commands.

Training for the show ring: An owner gently positions her young Boston Terrier, who appears to be loving the attention.

OVERCOMING PROBLEMS

It should be stressed that dogs who have problems with basic training do so for one of three reasons:

1. The dog has failed to understand the command that is being taught.

2. The owner has expected progress to be made too quickly.

3. The owner has failed to be consistent with the training sessions and/or the disciplinary corrections.

You will note that all three reasons have to do with the trainer rather than with the dog. If you find that your dog is not progressing, or is regressing, chances are that you tried to proceed to other commands before an earlier one was understood. For example, if a dog performs badly off the lead, this indicates that he was not up to standard on the lead.

In my experience, inconsistency is a major problem with many owners. They will give up on their dogs at times when they should be the most determined. In many instances, an owner will get fed up with walking his dog back to his original spot and will insist that the exercise is completed correctly. Or he will accept a sloppy or crooked sit, as long as the dog is sitting.

Another problem that is very common, especially with owners of large breeds, is that they fail to use the choke collar correctly. What happens is that the dog is allowed to lean into the collar, thus negating the whole basis of the choke effect. The dog soon learns that if he keeps the lead at full stretch, the choke will slide down to the base of his neck. The owner is then pulling at, rather than jerking, the collar. The effect is far less severe on the dog than on the owner, who is literally being hauled along.

Many owners cannot get themselves to give their dogs an abrupt pull because, quite naturally, they do not wish to hurt their dogs. However, no dog will walk to heel by its own choosing, so you are confronted with two simple situations: either the dog is given a few quick, sharp lessons that will make it very clear that if he pulls, he will get jerked backwards, or you must accept that for the rest of your dog's life you will be dragged around every time you take your pet out for a walk.

However, discipline should never be harsh when you are teaching basic commands. At

If your dog is missing the mark in training, review your techniques and your expectations. This Portuguese Water Dog has no trouble reeling in the line.

The relaxed, confident look on this Labrador's face shows that he is at ease by his owner's side and comfortable following her commands.

the most, punishment will be either the use of jerks on the choke, or a quick smack on the nose or rump. Timing is far more important than severity.

Correction must be progressive until you are able to establish the level needed for a given course of action to be implanted in your dog's brain. Conversely, we must tell the dog that he has achieved what we want by lavishing praise upon him.

PUNISHMENT PROBLEMS

Let's take a closer look at the effect of punishment on overcoming a given behavior pattern:

1. Extremes of punishment are rarely totally successful. If they achieve a change in behavior, they will almost certainly change the emotional state of the dog. They will greatly increase the risk of a neurotic or depressed dog.

2. The timing of punishment is crucial to effectiveness. It must be at the time of the incident. In this way, the dog is made aware that he can avoid the punishment by not doing that for which he is being punished. He alone controls the situation, so is able to determine events by his own actions.

3. Punishment must be consistent and not sporadic, otherwise the dog may not associate it with the undesirable action, even if it is given at the moment of the action.

4. Punishment must never be in conflict with an opposite alternative reaction from yourself. In other words, you cannot punish an action one time and praise it another (such as when the dog barks

The timing of corrections is everything. A Brittany runs alongside his master because he knows if he forges ahead he'll be pulled back.

The best solution to a problem is to avoid it altogether. By keeping puppies confined and on fresh newspapers, you don't have to worry about correcting them for having accidents.

at strangers when they approach your door, or if the dog jumps up on people).

5. Punishment should never be used if an alternate and less stressful correction will achieve the same desired behavioral change.

6. Whenever possible, punishment should not be associated with yourself. This does not mean someone else should do it, but merely that if the dog is to have a fear of an action, then it is better that it fears an object rather than you. However, the object should be chosen with care, both so it is not likely to injure the dog, and not to be generalized to other objects

the dog may be familiar with.

7. Punishment must bring rapid results, otherwise it will prove ineffective and risk adverse side effects.

8. You must try to remove all reinforcers that tend to maintain the undesirable behavior.

THE THROW CHAIN

Some trainers recommend using a throw chain, others don't. I do because a throw chain (or its equivalent) enables you to act on a problem as it happens and when it happens a short distance from you, making it difficult to discipline the dog. The throw chain offers the element of

surprise, and when it strikes the dog, he will not associate it with you. It does not unduly hurt the dog, yet it interrupts a misbehavior quite effectively. Finally, using a throw chain is a single action not likely to be excessive. It fulfills most of the needs for any corrective tool.

The throw chain does have drawbacks. There is always the risk that the dog may associate it with its choke chain training collar. However, as the one is placed on by you and the other arrives as if by magic (from the dog's point of view), it is unlikely that this association will become a major factor against its use. It

This Curly Coated Retriever knows it's training time when his choke collar goes on. This kind of collar can also be used to throw at a dog to startle him out of doing something bad, like running the fence.

is, of course, important that your aim is good, so it always strikes the dog on his hindquarters, and that the dog does not see you do the throwing.

Whatever object you use will carry the risk of association with something. If you are happier with something else, then maybe a can filled with pebbles will fit the need, although the rattling may alert the dog before the can strikes home. Marbles are another possibility, but they are potentially dangerous if your aim is not good. Occasions where throw chains will be effective are:

Garbage Rummaging. The best way to overcome this problem is to keep the garbage out of reach of the dog by either putting it under a counter or in a different room behind a closed door. If this is impossible, watch your dog carefully and place yourself so he will not see you throwing the chain. When he is very close to the trash can and makes his first move to dislodge the lid, throw the chain quite hard so it hits his rear end. This will startle him, and should hurt a little if it is to be effective. You must repeat this every time the dog approaches the trash, which means you must be present every time the dog has the opportunity to go to it. After each throw, you should appear and call the dog to you and give him lots of attention. Retrieve the chain when the dog's not looking.

Fence Running. Many dogs have the bad habit of running along their boundary fence and barking at passers-by. Have a friend who is a stranger to the dog walk by a few times. Conceal yourself and throw the chain when you

Dogs must be corrected while in the act of doing something undesirable. You can stage a situation where your dog will misbehave, like climbing on the furniture, so you can be there to correct him.

Steer your dog away from problem situations by diverting his attention with something he'll enjoy—like working for a treat. Use something tasty and highly digestible for your dog's sake. Photo courtesy of Nature's Recipe Pet Foods.

Garbage-can rummaging is a common problem that can be easily solved by keeping garbage can lids securely fastened and the cans themselves safely locked away.

Dogs like to be where the action is, and if people or other dogs pass by your fenced yard, it's difficult to keep your dog from running the fence. There are, however, methods you can try to break this habit.

are sure you will not miss the target. It will be worthwhile practicing throwing the chain before you actually use it on the dog, but do not let the dog see this! An alternative is to spray the dog with a hose as he starts to run the fence, but again you must be hidden from the dog so it comes as a shock when the cold water hits him.

A better correction for this problem would be to walk the dog at heel when people pass so he is in a counter-condi-

tioning situation (the dog cannot be at heel and run along the fence at the same time). Eventually the dog will become accustomed to seeing people pass by as he walks in the yard. You could then use the stern "Heel" command whenever the dog saw someone passing the fence.

Eating Feces. Again, you can use the throw chain if this is convenient. However, this problem may indicate a nutritional deficiency in the diet. Your veterinarian can

advise you on this matter. The problem may also have its roots in the dog's early life. If he was ever forced to sleep in close proximity to his own feces, he may have developed a liking or need for fecal matter. Only scrupulous cleanliness will eventually cure the problem.

With advice on the throw chain in mind, it is hoped you will understand that punishment is very rarely needed because there are nearly always alternatives. The biggest problem is that not everyone has the patience or understanding of problems to be prepared to devote the time necessary for retraining. These people are looking for the "quick fix," and faster usually means the level of discipline must increase in spite of the added risks this will entail.

BACK TO BASICS

Often, it is not understood that returning to basic training techniques will correct many problems seen in dogs. Basic training gives dogs something to occupy their minds, and it brings them into contact with other people and other dogs. There is no real shortcut to a well-behaved dog.

All training sessions should follow a set procedure. Play with your dog, then let him do a simple routine of exercises he knows well. Next, move on to a new command and finish when the dog understands the command and can be rewarded with praise. End the session with another play period. This sequence firmly fixes in the dog's mind that training will always start and end with fun. In between is the work period. Your dog will soon realize that if he does well during the work period, there is no displeasure involved at all. Once your dog has been trained, it is important to maintain his ability with regular practice.

Training for any number of activities---including showing in the ring---gives dogs something to occupy their minds, plus exposes them to more people and situations.

Dogs work hard to get what's pleasurable to them, and are expert beggars. If "no" isn't enough, some fair discipline early on will prevent a worse problem from developing.

DISCIPLINE

You will read and hear about people who think that a dog can be trained without punishment and that choke chains and prong collars are bestial and used only by overbearing bullies. Their opinions on what is cruel and what is not are based purely on the actual physical act of punishing a dog or any other animal. This is a naive attitude that is objectionable and results in problem dogs. You must, therefore, examine your inner feelings where dog training is concerned and accept reality. If you fail to train your dog, the dog will be the one who suffers. Unfortunately, you cannot train a dog on kindness alone. If you are not prepared to administer discipline, then forget about owning a dog, because you will run into problems. It would be quite impossible to train a dog any other way.

The art of training dogs lies not in whether punishment is

No matter how cute and cuddly they are, dogs cannot be trained on kindness alone. If this Pointer's owner doesn't want a lap dog forever, she'd better be firm about keeping her puppy on his bed on the floor.

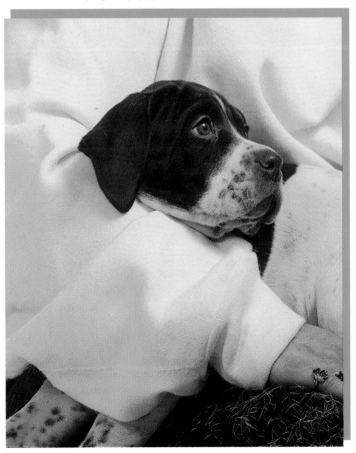

If he's not feeling well, your dog will not respond wholeheartedly to training. Feeding him a food that contains barley, pure lamb protein and wholesome grains (no wheat or corn), provides an excellent maintenance diet for all normally active adult dogs. Photo courtesy of Nature's Recipe Pet Foods.

to be used, but the extent of the punishment. The heavy-handed trainer can get fast results, but there is a big downside to such results—the dog becomes frightened of his owner. Remember, a dog should return to his owner with obvious enjoyment and with his tail held high and wagging. That tells you a lot about the way a dog has been trained.

An owner's personality and attitude will affect the way he

Genetics affect a dog's ability to do certain things. This Husky is a natural at weight pulling, but may need more time and training learning to track.

trains his dog, but what about the dog? Dogs are much more predictable than humans because they do not even think about the complexities of life in a human society. To them, life is a very simple matter of existing from day to day, and they just want to live peaceful and happy lives. To this end, they will do whatever is needed to try and please you, their substitute pack leader.

Not all dogs have the same capacity to learn, because we have taken some of their abilities away from them as a result of our breeding pro-grams. Intelligence, along with all other traits, is subject to genetic influence. Your dog is thus subject to certain limita-tions of its genes. Don't expect a Bull Terrier to be able to retrieve birds like a retriever, because it was never bred to retrieve. Even within a breed, a dog is very much an indi-vidual. Because your friend's German Shepherd is really top notch at tracking does not mean that yours will be.

It would be a mistake for you to have prior expectations of your dog's ability or the time it will take for you to train him. If you try to follow a schedule, you will become frustrated or annoyed if your dog does not adhere to the schedule. Your dog will sense your frustration, and from that point things can only go downhill.

You must appreciate the sort of dog you own so you know just how far you can and cannot go with him. His genetic potential is just that, potential. There are numerous things to consider in order to train your dog to his full potential. The effort really is worth it, because a well-trained dog is a very happy one.

Accept your dog for what he is and work with what you've got. Remember, he's a dog, and with that comes certain instinctive behaviors. Give him tough chew devices like Nylabones® to satisfy his instinct to gnaw.

In the Novice obedience class you will be expected to heel with your dog on leash at a fast pace, as shown, as well as at normal and slow paces.

APPENDIX I: REQUIREMENTS FOR THE NOVICE OBEDIENCE TEST

Heel on Leash and Figure Eight .... 40 points
*Forward * Halt * Right Turn * Left Turn * About Turn * Slow * Normal * Fast * Figure Eight*

Stand for Examination.. 30 points
*Stand Your Dog for Examination * Back to Your Dog * Exercise Finished*

Heel Free .... 40 points
*Forward * Halt * Right Turn * Left Turn * About Turn * Slow * Normal * Fast*

Recall .... 30 points
*Leave Your Dog * Call Your Dog * Finish*

Long Sit (One Minute) .... 30 points
*Sit Your Dog * Leave Your Dog * Back to Your Dog * Exercise Finished*

Long Down (Three Minutes) .... 30 points
*Down Your Dog * Leave Your Dog * Back to Your Dog * Exercise Finished*

Maximum Total Score: 200 points

Dogs that receive qualifying scores in Novice obedience under three different judges at three licensed or member obedience trials will earn a Companion Dog (CD) title.

The recall is another of the Novice obedience exercises you and your dog will need to do to earn a Companion Dog (CD) title.

APPENDIX II: REQUIREMENTS FOR THE OPEN OBEDIENCE TEST

Heel Free and Figure Eight .... 40 points
*Forward * Halt * Right Turn * Left Turn * About Turn * Slow * Normal * Fast * Figure Eight*

Drop on Recall... 30 points
*Leave Your Dog * Call Your Dog * Drop Your Dog * Call Your Dog * Finish*

Retrieve on Flat .... 20 points
*Throw Article * Send Your Dog * Take It * Finish*

Retrieve Over High Jump .... 30 points
*Throw Article * Send Your Dog * Take It * Finish*

Broad Jump .... 20 points
*Leave Your Dog * Send Your Dog * Finish*

Long Sit (Three Minutes) .... 30 points
*Sit Your Dog * Leave Your Dog * Back to Your Dog * Exercise Finished*

Long Down (Five Minutes) .... 30 points
*Down Your Dog * Leave Your Dog * Back to Your Dog * Finish*

Maximum Total Score: 200 points

Dogs that receive qualifying scores in Open obedience under three different judges at three licensed or member obedience trials will earn a Companion Dog Excellent (CDX) title.

A Golden Retriever soars over the broad jump in an Open obedience class.

APPENDIX III: REQUIREMENTS FOR THE UTILITY OBEDIENCE TEST

Signal Exercise .... 40 points
Using signals only, heel with Left Turn * Right Turn * About Turn * Halt * Slow * Normal * Fast * Stand Your Dog * Leave Your Dog * Signal to Drop, Sit, Come and Finish

Scent Discrimination, Article 1 .... 30 points
Send Your Dog * Take It * Finish

Scent Discrimination, Article 2 .... 30 points
Send Your Dog * Take It * Finish

Directed Retrieve .... 30 points
One, Two or Three * Take It * Finish

Moving Stand and Examination .... 30 points
Forward * Stand Your Dog * Call Your Dog to Heel

Directed Jumping .... 40 points
Send Your Dog * Bar or High * Finish

Maximum Total Score: 200 points

Dogs that receive qualifying scores in Utility obedience under three different judges at three licensed or member obedience trials will earn a Utility Dog (UD) title.

FOR MORE INFORMATION

The American Kennel Club can provide you with a training information brochure that provides a geographical listing of obedience and dog training clubs and information on the AKC's Canine Good Citizen program. Send your request for the brochure to:

The American Kennel Club
Fulfillment Department
5580 Centerview Dr.,
Suite 200
Raleigh, NC 27606-3390
Or call (919) 233-9780

In this Utility exercise (directed jumping), the handler has instructed his Golden to take the bar jump and return to him .

SUGGESTED READING

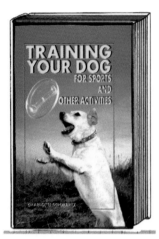

Training Your Dog For Sports and Other Activities

by Charlotte Schwartz

TS-258,

160 pages, over 200 full-color photographs. In this colorful and vividly illustrated book, author Charlotte Schwartz, a professional dog trainer for 40 years, demonstrates how your pet dog can assume a useful and meaningful role in everyday life. No matter what lifestyle you lead or what kind of dog you share your life with, there's a suitable and eye-opening activity in this book for you and your dog.

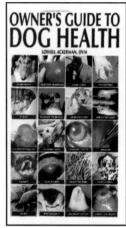

Owner's Guide to Dog Health

by Lowell Ackerman, DVM

TS-214

432 pages, over 300 color photographs. Winner of the 1995 Dog Writers Association of America's Best Health Book, this comprehensive title gives accurate, up-to-date information on all the major disorders and conditions found in dogs. Completely illustrated to help owners visualize signs of illness, different states of infection, procedures and treatment, it covers nutrition, skin disorders, disorders of the major body systems, dental health and more.

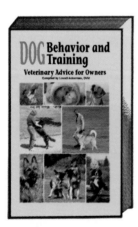

Dog Behavior and Training Veterinary Advice for Owners

TS-252

292 pages, over 200 color photographs. Joined by co-editors Gary Landsberg, DVM, and Wayne Hunthausen, DVM, Dr. Lowell Ackerman and about 20 experts in behavioral studies and training set forth a practical guide to the common problems owners experience with their dogs. Since behavioral disorders are the number-one reason for owners to abandon a dog, it is essential for owners to understand how the dog thinks and how to correct him if he misbehaves.

The Most Complete Dog Book Ever Written (A Canine Lexicon)

by Andrew De Prisco and James B. Johnson

TS-175

896 pages, over 1300 full-color photographs. This book is an up-to-date encyclopedic dictionary for the dog person. It is the most complete single volume on the dog ever published, covering more dog breeds than any other book, as well as other relevant topics including health, showing, training, breeding, veterinary terms and much more.